To: _____

With true affection.

From: _____

The Helen Steiner Rice Foundation

Whatever the celebration, whatever the day, whatever the event, whatever the occasion, Helen Steiner Rice possessed the ability to express the appropriate feeling for that particular moment in time. A happening became happier, a sentiment more sentimental, a memory more memorable because of her deep sensitivity and ability to put into understandable language the emotion being experienced. Her positive attitude, her concern for others, and her love of God are identifiable threads woven into her life, her work ... and even her death.

Prior to Mrs. Rice's passing, she established the HELEN STEINER RICE FOUNDATION, a nonprofit corporation that awards grants to worthy charitable programs assisting the elderly and the needy.

Royalties from the sale of this book will add to the financial capabilities of the HELEN STEINER RICE FOUNDATION. Because of limited resources, the foundation presently restricts grants to qualified charitable programs in Lorain, Ohio, where Helen Steiner Rice was born, and Greater Cincinnati, Ohio, where Mrs. Rice lived and worked most of her life.

Because of her foresight, caring, and deep convictions of sharing, Helen Steiner Rice continues to touch a countless number of lives through foundation grants and her inspirational poetry.

Thank you for your assistance in helping to keep Helen's dream alive and growing.

ANDREA E. CORNETT, ADMINISTRATOR

Gifts
of
Love

Second Edition

Helen Steiner Rice
and Virginia J. Ruehlmann

Fleming H. Revell
A Division of Baker Book House Co
Grand Rapids, Michigan 49516

Published by Fleming H. Revell
a division of Baker Book House Company
P.O. Box 6287, Grand Rapids, MI 49516-6287

Printed in the United States of America

Library of Congress Cataloging-in-Publication Data

Rice, Helen Steiner.
    Gifts of love / Helen Steiner Rice and Virginia J. Ruehlmann.—2nd ed.
        p. cm.
      ISBN 0-8007-1770-8 (cloth)
        1. Christian poetry, American. 2. Love poetry, American.
    I. Ruehlmann, Virginia J. II. Title.
    [PS3568.I28G544 1999]
    811´.54—dc21   99-42717

Unless otherwise indicated, Scripture quotations are from the HOLY BIBLE, NEW INTERNATIONAL VERSION®. NIV®. Copyright © 1973, 1978, 1984 by International Bible Society. Used by permission of Zondervan Publishing House. All rights reserved.

Scripture quotations identified RSV are from the Revised Standard Version of the Bible, copyright 1946, 1952, 1971 by the Division of Christian Education of the National Council of the Churches of Christ in the USA. Used by permission.

Sincere appreciation is expressed to Florence Doogan Juergens and Virginia Juergens Ruehlmann for the use of valentines from their antique card collection.

A special thank you to Ruth Waybrant and Janet McCann Robinson for allowing us to use their linens and lace for background decoration.

Interior design by Robin Black.

For current information about all releases from Baker Book House, visit our web site:
http://www.bakerbooks.com

Dedicated to
all who seek or share love
and to those who live
a love-filled life

I life bear for you
its sweetest flowers

Trust to me.

Contents

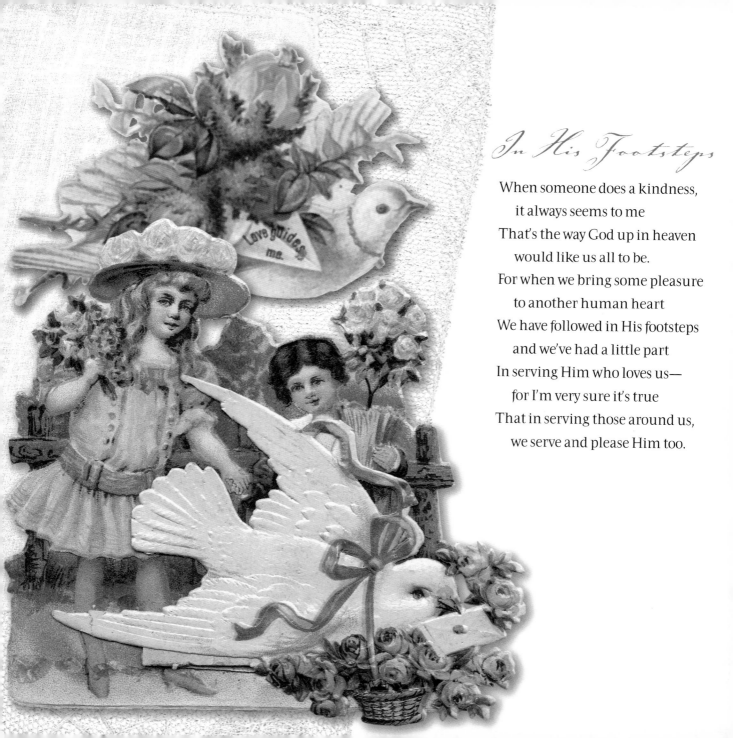

In His Footsteps

When someone does a kindness,
   it always seems to me
That's the way God up in heaven
   would like us all to be.
For when we bring some pleasure
   to another human heart
We have followed in His footsteps
   and we've had a little part
In serving Him who loves us—
   for I'm very sure it's true
That in serving those around us,
   we serve and please Him too.

Introduction

For centuries lyricists and poets have recounted, recited, related, and reported the virtues and characteristics of love. Verses, plays, songs, even nursery rhymes and valentines have extolled the attributes of those in love. Descriptions of love vary from "a many-splendored thing" that "walks right in and chases clouds away," to a true love that is "stronger than the highest mountain, deeper than the deepest sea." We are told that at times love can be as "elusive as a butterfly," but it "makes the world go round." These phrases, of course, all refer to a romantic type of love.

A true understanding of the many varieties of love is found in the Bible, where love is defined, explained, and explored. Using the Scriptures as her principle and goal, Helen Steiner Rice not only lived a life based on love but wrote, in beautiful phrases and rhyming verse, of loves that are patient, kind, understanding, and forgiving—namely, God's love for us and our love for God, love between neighbors and friends, love between sweethearts, love between man and wife, love of parents, and love within a family.

Love in any language is appreciated, valued, longed for, needed, and, hopefully, expressed. Who among us does not thrive and feel happier on hearing the words "I love you" addressed to our ears and heart by a child, a parent, a friend, a spouse?

So let love—agape, familial, friendly, marital, neighborly, parental, romantic, spiritual, and unconditional—thrive and live on!

Lovingly,
Virginia J. Ruehlmann

To my
Valentine

Love—the Priceless Gift

Love is something eternal—the aspect may change, but not the essence. There is the same difference in a person before and after he is in love as there is in an unlighted lamp and one that is burning. The lamp was there and it was a good lamp, but now it is shedding light, too, and that is its real function.

VINCENT VAN GOGH

Wings of Love

The priceless gift of life is love,
    for with the help of God above,
Love can change the human race
    and make this world a better place.
For love dissolves all hate and fear
    and makes our vision bright and clear
So we can see and rise above
    our pettiness on wings of love.

*Life is a magic vase filled to the brim; so made that
you cannot dip into nor draw from it; but it overflows into
the hand that drops treasures into it—drop in malice and
it overflows hate; drop in charity and it overflows love.*

JOHN RUSKIN

I Love You

I love you for so many things,
    I don't know where to start,
But most of all I love you
    for your understanding heart—
A heart that makes you thoughtful
    and considerate and kind,
A heavenly combination
    that is difficult to find.
And I can't help the feeling
    that loving folks like you
Sent out so many thought waves
    that my dearest dream came true.

I like not only to be loved, but to be told that I am loved; the realm of silence is large enough beyond the grave.

GEORGE ELIOT

13

A Gift

Love is a gift
  to treasure forever
Given by God
  without price tag or measure.
Love is a gift
  we can all possess,
Love is a key
  to the soul's happiness!

Love cannot be forced, love cannot be coaxed and teased. It comes out of Heaven, unmasked and unsought.

PEARL BUCK

Priceless Gifts

This brings you a million good wishes and more
For the things you cannot buy in a store—
A joy-filled heart and a happy smile,
Faith to sustain you in times of trial,
Contentment, inner peace, and love—
All priceless gifts from God above!

Constant Love

Rings and jewels are not gifts, but apologies for gifts. The only true gift is a portion of thyself.

RALPH WALDO EMERSON

15

What Is Love?

What is love?
   No words can define it—
It's something so great
   only God could design it.
Wonder of wonders,
   beyond our conception,
And only in God
   can love find true perfection.
For love means much more
   than small words can express,
For what we call love
   is so very much less
Than the beauty and depth
   and the true richness of
God's gift to mankind—
   His compassionate love.
For love has become
   a word that's misused,
Perverted, distorted,
   and often abused
To speak of light romance
   or some affinity for

A passing attraction
that is seldom much more
Than a mere interlude
or inflamed fascination,
A romantic fling
of no lasting duration.
But love is enduring
and patient and kind,
It judges all things
with the heart, not the mind.
For love is unselfish—
giving more than it takes—
And no matter what happens,
love never forsakes.
It's faithful and trusting
and always believing,
Guileless and honest
and never deceiving.
Yes, love is beyond
what we can define,
For love is immortal
and God's gift is divine.

Love Works in Wondrous Ways

With love in our hearts,
 let us try this year
To lift the clouds
 of hate and fear,
For love works in ways
 that are wondrous and strange,
And there is nothing in life
 that love cannot change.

Who, being loved, is poor?
OSCAR WILDE

Loving Greeting

With L...

18

The Magic of Love

Love is like magic
 and it always will be,
For love still remains
 life's sweet mystery.
Love works in ways
 that are wondrous and strange,
And there's nothing in life
 that love cannot change.
Love can transform
 the most commonplace
Into beauty and splendor
 and sweetness and grace.

Love is unselfish,
 understanding, and kind,
For it sees with its heart
 and not with its mind.
Love is the answer
 that everyone seeks.
Love is the language
 that every heart speaks.
Love can't be bought—
 it's priceless and free.
Love, like pure magic,
 is a sweet mystery.

*Let no man think he is loved by any man
when he loves no man.*

EPICTETUS

19

The True Gift

With our hands we give gifts
    that money can buy—
Diamonds that sparkle
    like stars in the sky,
Trinkets that glitter
    like the sun as it rises,
Beautiful baubles
    that come as surprises—
But only our hearts
    can feel real love
And share the gift
    of our Father above.

*'Tis sweet to feel by what fine-spun threads
our affections are drawn together.*

LAURENCE STERNE

20

LOVE'S GREETING

All that I have, all that is mine,
I'll share with you, my Valentine.

Remember This

Great is the power of might and mind,
    but only love can make us kind,
And all we are or hope to be
    is empty pride and vanity.
If love is not a part of all,
    the greatest man is very small.

Let all bitterness and wrath and anger and clamor and slander be put away from you, with all malice, and be kind to one another, tenderhearted, forgiving one another, as God in Christ forgave you.

EPHESIANS 4:31-32 RSV

21

The Garden of Friendship

Dear friends, let us love one another, for love comes from God. Everyone who loves has been born of God and knows God.

1 JOHN 4:7

Give Lavishly!

The more you give,
the more you get;
The more you laugh,
the less you fret.
The more you do
unselfishly,
The more you live
abundantly.
The more of everything
you share,

The more you'll always
have to spare.
The more you love,
the more you'll find
That life is good
and friends are kind.
For only what
we give away
Enriches us
from day to day.

*To love abundantly is to live abundantly,
and to love forever is to live forever.*

AUTHOR UNKNOWN

Trust to me.

24

The Key to Living

Every day is a reason for giving,
And giving is the key to living.
So let us give ourselves away,
Not just today but every day,
And remember, a kind and thoughtful deed
Or a hand outstretched in a time of need
Is the rarest of gifts, for it is a part
Not of the purse but a loving heart,
And he who gives of himself will find
True joy of heart and peace of mind.

Be unselfish. That is the first and final commandment for those who would be useful and happy in their usefulness. If you think of yourself only, you cannot develop because you are choking the source of development, which is spiritual expansion through thought for others.

CHARLES W. ELIOT

25

Happiness Grows

You cannot bring happiness

into the lives of others

without spreading

a little of it

inside your own heart.

He who would have beautiful roses in his garden must have beautiful roses in his heart. He must love them well and always. He must have not only the glowing admiration, the enthusiasm, and the passion, but the tenderness, the thoughtfulness, the reverence, the watchfulness of love.

S. R. HOLE

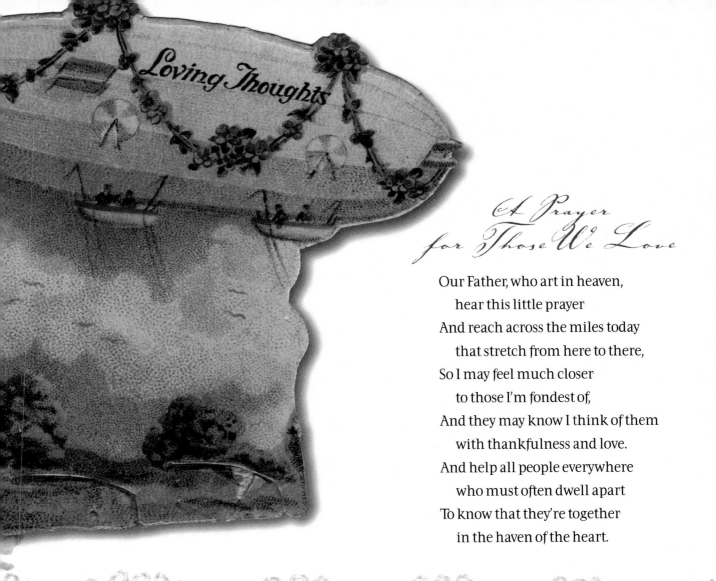

Loving Thoughts

A Prayer for Those We Love

Our Father, who art in heaven,
  hear this little prayer
And reach across the miles today
  that stretch from here to there,
So I may feel much closer
  to those I'm fondest of,
And they may know I think of them
  with thankfulness and love.
And help all people everywhere
  who must often dwell apart
To know that they're together
  in the haven of the heart.

We are most of us very lonely in this world; you who have any who love you, cling to them and thank God.

WILLIAM MAKEPEACE THACKERAY

TO MY VALENTINE

Everyone Needs Someone

People need people,
and friends need friends,
And we all need love,
for a full life depends
Not on vast riches
or great acclaim,
Not on success
or worldly fame,
But just on knowing
that someone cares
And holds us close
in thoughts and prayers,
For only the knowledge
that we're understood
Makes everyday living
feel wonderfully good.

And we rob ourselves
of life's greatest need
When we lock up our hearts
and fail to heed
The outstretched hand
reaching to find
A kindred spirit
whose heart and mind
Are lonely and longing
to somehow share
Our joys and sorrows
and to make us aware
That life's completeness
and richness depend
On the things we share
with our loved ones and friends.

Believe my love is sincere.

29

Garden of Friendship

No garden is ever really complete
Without a rose to make it sweet.
No life is ever full or fair
Without someone to share and care!

There is no garden so complete
But roses could make the place more sweet.
There is no life so rich and rare
But one more friend can enter there.

A good deed is never lost; he who sows courtesy reaps friendship, and he who plants kindness gathers love.
SAINT BASIL

Those Who Are Nice to Know

There are some that we meet in passing
    and forget them as soon as they go;
There are some we remember with pleasure
    because they are so nice to know.
There are those who at first seem appealing,
    whose ethics and standards seem high,
But slowly we grow disillusioned,
    and esteem and respect fade and die.
But it is surely refreshing
    to find in this wide world today
People who grow even greater
    in all that they do and they say.

To stand strong graciously;
to smile sincerely; to love always;
and to seek understanding—
these are the worthy ambitions
of a life worth living.

ESTHER FRESHMAN

31

Romance—
Deep within the Heart

*No cord or cable can draw so forcibly, or bind so fast,
as love can do with a single thread.*

ROBERT BURTON

A Priceless Treasure

Love is like a priceless treasure,
　　which there is no way to measure,
For who can fathom stars or sea
　　or figure the length of eternity?
Love's too great to understand,
　　but just to clasp a loved one's hand
Can change the darkness into light
　　and make the heart take wingless flight,
And blessed are they who walk in love,
　　for love's a gift from God above.

*For where your treasure is,
there your heart will be also.*

MATTHEW 6:21

34

Love's Test

Dear God,
Please help me in my feeble way
To somehow do something each day
To show the one I love the best
My faith in him will stand each test.
And let me show in some small way
The love I have for him each day
And prove beyond all doubt and fear
That his love for me I hold most dear.
And so I ask of God above—
Just make me worthy of his love.

Love cannot endure indifference. It needs to be wanted. Like a lamp, it needs to be fed out of the oil of another's heart, or its flame burns low.

HENRY WARD BEECHER

To the one I love

Sweetheart

Deep in My Heart

Happy little memories
  go flitting through my mind,
And in all my thoughts and memories
  I always seem to find
The picture of your face, dear,
  the memory of your touch,
And all the other little things
  I've come to love so much.
You cannot go beyond my thoughts
  or leave my love behind,
Because I keep you in my heart
  and forever in my mind.
And though I may not tell you,
  I think you know it's true
That I find daily happiness
  in the very thought of you.

Memory, of all the powers of the mind, is the most delicate and frail.

BEN JONSON

If I Had Loved You Then

If I had known you way back when,
  I might have loved you even then,
But, oh, what a difference there would have been
  if instead of now, I'd loved you then.
Our love might have burned with a brighter flame,
  we'd have toasted our fame in bubbling champagne,
We'd have loved and been lost in a world of fun,
  and now our young love would be over and done.
But meeting each other in the gold, autumn haze
  has brought deeper meaning to the last, golden days.

*Every year I live I am more convinced that the
waste of life lies in the love we have not given; the
powers we have not used; the selfish prudence
which will risk nothing and which, shrinking pain,
misses happiness as well.*

JOHN B. TABB

To Franklin

In my eyes there lies no vision
    but the sight of your dear face,
In my heart there is no feeling
    but the warmth of your embrace,
In my mind there are no thoughts
    but thoughts of you, my dear,
In my soul, no other longing
    but just to have you near.
All my dreams are built around you,
    and I've come to know it's true—
In my life there is no living
    that is not a part of you.

My bounty is as boundless as the sea, my love is deep; the more I give to thee, the more I have, for both are infinite.

WILLIAM SHAKESPEARE

38

A token of Love

Printed in Germany

A Night Song

In the night I send a song—
    that song, dear, is of you.
Every soul is crying out
    a message just for you.
The stars up in the heaven,
    they seem to understand—
They know that I am calling
    into a far-off land.
The clouds glide by in glory—
    they smile at me and say
That you are thinking of me too,
    in just the same sweet way.

Merrily the moon winks on—
    it winked at you, I know—
For the greeting that it gave me
    was just enough to show
Old nighttime brings me nearer
    to one I love so well,
And twinkling stars and moonbeams
    ne'er get a chance to tell.
And although we are far apart,
    your face I almost see,
For stars that take your message
    are smiling back at me.

*For those who love,
time is eternity.*
HENRY VAN DYKE

To my Valentine

39

If I Could Tell You

It's such a quiet, lovely thing,
    it doesn't ask for much.
It isn't untamed longing
    that cries for passion's touch.
It's not built upon the quicksand
    of a pair of lips and arms,
For only false foundations
    are raised on physical charms.
I wish that I could tell you
    about this thing I feel,
It's intangible like gossamer,
    but like a hoop of steel

It binds me very close to you
    and opens up the door
To more real, deep contentment
    than I've ever known before.
You see, your music reaches
    beyond where words dare pass,
It's like a soul's communion
    or a sacred, holy mass.
It's something indefinable,
    like a sea and sky and sod—
It might just be enchantment,
    but I like to think it's God.

To love and be loved is to feel the sun from both sides.

DAVID VISCOTT

May Thy Path Be Ever Blest.

The Joys of Remembering

There's a heap of satisfaction
    to sit here thinking of you
And to tell you once again, dear,
    how very much I love you.
There is comfort just in longing
    for a smile from your face
And joy in just remembering
    each sweet and fond embrace.
There is happiness in knowing
    that my heart will always be
A place where I can hold you
    and keep you near to me.

It is through a growing awareness that you stock and enrich your memory ... and as a great philosopher has said: "A man thinks with his memory."

WILFRED A. PETERSON

41

Happiness

You put the *love* in loveliness
 and the *sweet* in sweetness too.
I think they took life's dearest things
 and wrapped them up in you.
And when I send good wishes,
 they're filled with love so true,
And I hope the year will bring you
 the joy that is your due.
For when I think of you, dear,
 I can't forget the thought
Of how much real, true happiness
 just knowing you has brought.

Thank God for memory, that most gracious artist, who softens the hard things in our lives, and makes more beautiful the beautiful ones. It gilds the faces of those who have gone, with a radiance we could never see whilst we had them here, and makes the "waste places in our lives to blossom as the rose."

AUTHOR UNKNOWN

Remembrance Road

There's a road I call remembrance
    where I walk each day with you.
It's a pleasant, happy road, my dear,
    all filled with memories true.
Today it leads me through a spot
    where I can dream a while,
And in its tranquil peacefulness
    I touch your hand and smile.
There are hills and fields and budding trees
    and stillness that's so sweet
That it seems that this must be the place
    where God and humans meet.
I hope we can go back again
    and golden hours renew,
And God go with you always, dear,
    until the day we do.

*Of all the music that reached far-
thest into heaven, it is the beating
of a loving heart.*

HENRY WARD BEECHER

Valentines—
Communion of Hearts

Love sought is good, but given unsought is better.

WILLIAM SHAKESPEARE

What Are Valentines?

Valentines are gifts of love,
and with the help of God above,
Love can change the human race
and make this world a better place …
For love dissolves all hate and fear
and makes our vision bright and clear
So we can see and rise above
our pettiness on wings of love.

*Lord, make me an instrument of
Thy peace, where there is hatred, let me
sow love. Where there is injury, pardon.*
SAINT FRANCIS OF ASSISI

46

My Love for You

There are things we cannot measure,
　　like the depths of waves and sea
And the heights of stars in heaven
　　and the joy you bring to me.
Like eternity's long endlessness
　　and the sunset's golden hue,
There is no way to measure
　　the love I have for you.

To be happy is not to possess much,
but to hope and to love much.

FELICITÉ ROBERT DE LAMENNAIS

47

The Legend of Saint Valentine

The story of Saint Valentine
   is a legend, it is true,
But legends are delightful
   and very lovely too.
The legend says Saint Valentine,
   imprisoned in a cell,
Was thinking of his little flock
   he had always loved so well.
He wanted to assure them
   of his friendship and his love,
So he picked a bunch of violets
   and sent them by a dove.
And on the violets' velvet leaves
   he pierced these lines divine—
They simply said, "I love you
   and I'm your Valentine."

So through the years that followed
   from that day unto this,
Folks still send messages of love
   and seal them with a kiss,
Because a saint in prison
   reached outside his bars one day
And picked a bunch of violets
   and sent them out to say
That faith and love can triumph
   no matter where you are,
For faith and love are greater
   than the strongest prison bar.

In Your Heart

Keep me in your heart, dear,
and in your every prayer,
For wherever you are, darling,
I like to feel I'm there.

*Love is never lost. If not
reciprocated, it will flow back
and soften and purify the heart.*
WASHINGTON IRVING

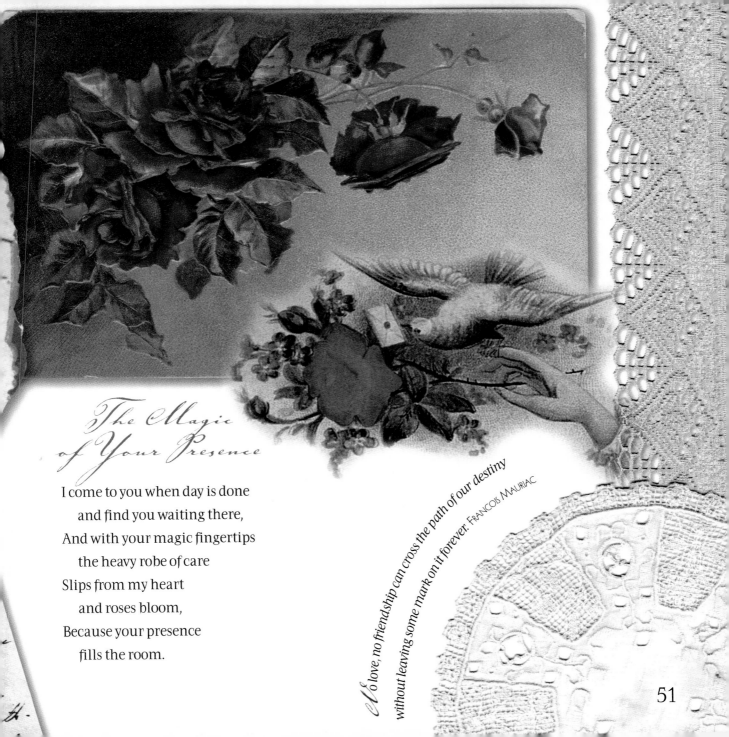

The Magic of Your Presence

I come to you when day is done
and find you waiting there,
And with your magic fingertips
the heavy robe of care
Slips from my heart
and roses bloom,
Because your presence
fills the room.

No love, no friendship can cross the path of our destiny without leaving some mark on it forever. FRANÇOIS MAURIAC

51

St. Valentine's Day Customs

Many curious customs are associated with St. Valentine's Day. In early England it was a tradition for a young girl to pin fresh bay leaves on her pillow before retiring on the eve of St. Valentine's Day. A dream of her sweetheart confirmed that they would marry.

Another old English tradition was "valentining." On the morning of St. Valentine's Day, groups of children would go from house to house serenading the residents. In turn, they would receive gifts of coins and candies.

Early valentines in England were written by hand and personally decorated by the sender. Each year a collection of sentimental verses on topics ranging from friendship to love was published. From this

CUPID'S L?

Head Offices
True Heart Lane,
Branches in all Countries.
Specialists
in Affairs of the Heart.

To my Valentine

	Kisses.
Feb 14 To supplying Golden Key	5
Unlocking heart that beats for Thee,	15
Forging Lovers links and Token	10
Ensuring they shall ne'er be broken	8
Supplying also Love's cement	4
Including time so sweetly spent.	12
	54

Payment prompt of this is claimed,
No discount can be Entertained.

To my VALENTINE.

Cupid's Message

Valentine Writers Handbook, a person selected an appropriate verse, copied it by hand onto a piece of stationery, and embellished it with hand-drawn designs or cutout pictures. Around 1825, embossed papers and fancy valentines were being manufactured in England.

A woman named Esther Howland, daughter of a Worcester, Massachusetts, stationer, was the first person to manufacture valentines in America. Miss Howland, a graduate of Mount Holyoke Seminary, received a commercially made valentine from England in 1849. It was the first she had ever seen, and she promptly decided she could improve on the product. She ordered lace, sheets of colored paper, and paper flowers and created several designs to use as samples. She was amazed at the response and the number of orders that poured in. For well over fifty years, Miss Howland controlled the entire valentine industry in America.

V.J.R.

To my Valentine

Cable Message
THE WESTERN UNION TELEGRAPH COMPANY

A Valentine Message.

A token of Affection

Across the Miles

I think of you so many times
    and wish with all my heart
That I could reach across the miles
    that keep us far apart
And somehow just communicate
    the things I'd like to say
If I were standing close to you
    instead of far away.

*The heart that has truly
loved never forgets but as
truly loves on to the close.*

THOMAS MORE

54

Memories

You are the kind of a person
    who leaves lovely memories behind
Of goodness and sweetness and beauty
    that glow from the face, heart, and mind.

*Memory was given to mortals so that
they might have roses in December.*

AUTHOR UNKNOWN

To One I Love

The Gift of Lasting Love

For this reason a man will leave his father and mother and be united to his wife, and they will become one flesh.

GENESIS 2:24

What Is Marriage?

It is sharing and caring,
giving and forgiving,
loving and being loved,
walking hand in hand,
talking heart to heart,
seeing through each other's eyes,
laughing together,
weeping together,
praying together,
and always trusting and believing
and thanking God for each other.
For love that is shared is a beautiful thing,
It enriches the soul and makes the heart sing.

ST. VALENTINE'S GREE

I love you, little
Sweetheart mine,
And want you for
my Valentine.

Love bears all things, believes all things, hopes all things, endures all things.
1 CORINTHIANS 13:7 RSV

To my Valentine

The Joy of Love

Love is a many-splendored thing,
the greatest joy that life can bring,
And let no one try to disparage
the sacred bond of holy marriage,
For love is not love until God above
sanctifies the union of two people in love.

Treasure the love you receive above all.
It will survive long after your gold and
good health have vanished.

OG MANDINO

When Two People Marry

Your hearts are filled with happiness
    so great and overflowing
You cannot comprehend it,
    for it's far beyond all knowing
How any heart could hold such joy
    or feel the fullness of
The wonder and the glory
    and the ecstasy of love.
You wish that you could capture it
    and never let it go
So you might walk forever
    in its magic, radiant glow.
And love in all its ecstasy
    is such a fragile thing,
Like gossamer in cloudless skies
    or a hummingbird's small wing.
And love that lasts forever
    must be made of something strong—
The kind of strength that's gathered
    when the heart can hear no song,
When the sunshine of your wedding day
    runs into stormy weather,

And hand in hand you brave the gale
    and climb steep hills together,
And, clinging to each other
    while the thunder rolls above,
You seek divine protection
    in faith and hope and love.
For days of wine and roses
    never make love's dreams come true—
It takes sacrifice and teardrops
    and problems shared by two
To give true love its beauty,
    its grandeur, and its finesse,
And to mold an earthly ecstasy
    into heavenly divineness.

Loving Greeting.

Lasting Love

Love is much more than a tender caress
and more than bright hours of happiness,
For a lasting love is made up of sharing
both hours that are joyous and also despairing.
It's made up of patience and deep understanding
and never of stubborn or selfish demanding.
It's made up of climbing the steep hills together
and facing with courage life's stormiest weather.
Nothing on earth or in heaven can part
a love that has grown to be part of the heart,
And just like the sun and the stars and sea,
this love will go on through eternity,
For true love lives on when earthly things die,
for it's part of the spirit that soars to the sky.

*Though love seems the fastest of all growths,
it is really the slowest. No man or woman knows
what perfect love is, until they have been married
a quarter of a century.*

MARK TWAIN

62

Married couples who love each other tell each other a thousand things without talking.
CHINESE PROVERB

When I Married You

When I married you, my darling,
   I loved you very much—
I thrilled to have you near me
    and at the dearness of your touch.
I said no love could ever be
    more wonderful than this
And no thrill could ever equal
    the magic of your kiss.
But, darling, I've discovered
    that I really never knew
That anyone could love someone
    the way I now love you.
For God has blessed our union
    with the miracle of love
And given us this little child
    that we are guardians of,
And so, together, sweetheart,
    we've a deeper joy to share,
For God has just entrusted
    a small angel to our care.

Engagement and Wedding Customs

In early times, betrothal rings of wood and leather were popular, and in ancient Ireland, it was customary for a man to present a ring or bracelet woven of human hair to the woman he wished to marry. In A.D. 869, Pope Nicholas decreed that a ring made of precious metal would become the official statement of nuptial intent. Both the bracelet and the ring are circles, symbolizing a never-ending union.

In the fifteenth century, diamonds became a part of the ring's setting, and within a hundred years, a diamond ring became the most accepted and sought after statement of betrothal.

Engagement and wedding rings are traditionally worn on the fourth digit on the left hand. In ancient times, it was thought that a particular blood vessel and nerve ran directly from that finger to the heart. Of course, the heart was considered the location of affections. Through the years, this concept has been challenged from an anatomical perspective, but that finger has remained the "ring finger." A less romantic and far more practical explanation is that the ring finger is the least used and also most protected finger.

The custom of throwing rice at the departing bridal couple also dates back to ancient times. Rice, symbolic of fertility, was used to wish fruitfulness for the newly married couple. In countries in which rice was not readily available, nuts, wheat, and barley were thrown or strewn after the ceremony.

V.J.R.

Honeymoon

The term *honeymoon* refers to the first month after a wedding, a time in which the bride and groom adjust to their new state of matrimony. This period of time received its name from a drink known as mead, which, in the early years of England, was served to the bride and groom at their wedding celebration and also before retiring every night for a full cycle of the moon. Mead, a fermented liquor with a base made of an abundance of honey, some water, and a few spices, was considered a fertility drink, and its consumption guaranteed the couple offspring. Combine the word *honey* from the mead with the cycle of the *moon,* and the word *honeymoon* is the result.

V.J.R.

May God Bless Your Wedding Day

May God bless your wedding day
    and every day thereafter
And fill your home with happiness
    and your hearts with love and laughter.
And may each year together
    find you more and more in love
And bring you all the happiness
    you're so deserving of.
May the joy of true companionship
    be yours to share through life,
And may you always bless the day
    that made you husband and wife.

The spectrum of love has nine ingredients: patience, kindness, generosity, humility, courtesy, unselfishness, good temper, guilelessness, and sincerity.

HENRY DRUMMOND

66

Anniversary Thoughts

It takes a special day like this
  to just look back and reminisce
And think of things you used to do
  when love was young and so were you.
But all things change, for that is life,
  and love between a man and wife
Cannot remain romantic bliss
  forever flavored with a kiss.
But always there's the bond of love
  that there is no explaining of,
And through the trials of life it grows
  like flowers do beneath the snows.

Sometimes it's hidden from the sight
  just like the sun gives way to night,
But always there's that bond of love
  that there is no explaining of.
And every year that you're together,
  regardless of the kind of weather,
That bond of love keeps growing stronger
  because you've shared it one year longer.
And it's a pleasure I wouldn't miss,
  wishing you joy on a day like this,
And may the good Lord up above
  look down today and bless your love.

To the one I love.

There is a land of the living and a land of the dead, and the bridge is love.
THORNTON WILDER

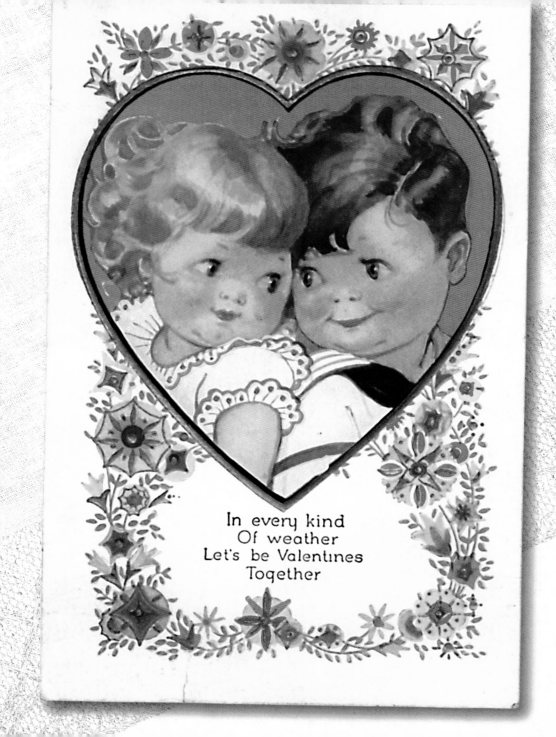

In every kind
Of weather
Let's be Valentines
Together

Family—
the Secure Haven

*Love is an active power, a power which breaks
through the walls which separate man from his fellow
man. Love overcomes the sense of isolation and sepa-
rateness, yet it permits you to be yourself. In love the
paradox occurs that two beings become one and yet
remain two.*

ERICH FROMM

A Mother's Love

A mother's love is something
    that no one can explain—
It is made of deep devotion
    and of sacrifice and pain.
It is endless and unselfish
    and enduring, come what may,
For nothing can destroy it
    or take the love away.
It is patient and forgiving
    when all others are forsaking,
And it never fails or falters
    even though the heart is breaking.

It believes beyond believing
    when the world around condemns,
And it glows with all the beauty
    of the rarest, brightest gems.
It is far beyond defining,
    it defies all explanation,
And it still remains a secret
    like the mysteries of creation—
A many-splendored miracle
    we cannot understand
And another wondrous evidence
    of God's tender, guiding hand.

*Life is a flame that is always burning itself out,
but it catches fire again every time a child is born.*

GEORGE BERNARD SHAW

Dads are special people
no home should be without,
For every family will agree
they're so nice to have about.
They are a happy mixture
of a small boy and a man,
And they're very necessary
in every family plan.
Sometimes they're most demanding
and stern and firm and tough,
But underneath they're soft as silk,
for this is just a bluff.

For in any kind of trouble
Dad reaches out his hand,
And you can always count on him
to help and understand.
And while we do not praise Dad
as often as we should,
We love him and admire him,
and while that's understood,
It's only fair to emphasize
his importance and his worth,
For if there were no loving dads,
this would be a loveless earth.

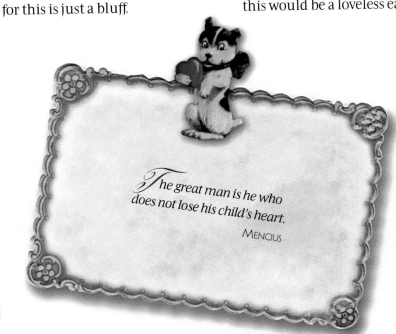

The great man is he who does not lose his child's heart.

MENCIUS

A token of Affection

A token
of
affection

Germany

Loving Thoughts

Fathers Are Wonderful People

Fathers are wonderful people,
    too little understood,
And we do not sing their praises
    as often as we should.
For somehow Father seems to be
    the man who pays the bills,
While Mother binds up little hurts
    and nurses all our ills.
And Father struggles daily
    to live up to his image
As protector and provider
    and the hero of the scrimmage.
And perhaps that is the reason
    we sometimes get the notion
That fathers are not subject
    to the thing we call emotion,

But if you look inside Dad's heart,
   where no one else can see,
You'll find he's sentimental
   and as soft as he can be.
But he's so busy every day
   in the grueling race of life
That he leaves the sentimental stuff
   to his partner and his wife.
But fathers are just wonderful
   in a million different ways
And they merit loving compliments
   and accolades of praise,
For the only reason Dad aspires
   to fortune and success
Is to make the family proud of him
   and to bring them happiness.
And like our heavenly Father,
   he's a guardian and guide,
Someone we can count on
   to be always on our side.

Motherhood

The dearest gifts that heaven holds,
    the very finest too,
Were made into one pattern
    that was perfect, sweet, and true.
The angels smiled, well pleased, and said,
    "Compared to all the others,
This pattern is so wonderful
    let's use it just for mothers!"
And through the years, a mother
    has been all that's sweet and good,
For there's a bit of God and love
    in all true motherhood.

*When God thought of Mother, he must
have laughed with satisfaction, and framed it
quickly—so rich, so deep, so divine, so full of
soul power, and beauty, was the conception!*

HENRY WARD BEECHER

74

Mother Is a Word Called Love

Mother is a word called love,
  and all the world is mindful of
That the love that's given and shown to others
  is different from the love of mothers.
For mothers play the leading roles
  in giving birth to little souls—
For though small souls are heaven-sent
  and we realize they're only lent,
It takes a mother's loving hands
  and her gentle heart that understands
To mold and shape this little life
  and shelter it from storm and strife.
No other love than mother love
  could do the things required of
The one to whom God gives the keeping
  of His wee lambs, awake or sleeping.
So mothers are a special race
  God sent to earth to take His place.

Babies are bits of stardust
blown from the hand of God.
Lucky the woman who
knows the pangs of birth
for she has held a star.
LARRY BARRETTO

Cling to my heart—
my Valentine

To my
Valentine

Made in Germany

A Mother's Love Is a Haven

A mother's love is like an island
    in life's ocean vast and wide—
A peaceful, quiet shelter
    from the restless, rising tide.
A mother's love is like a fortress,
    and we seek protection there
When the waves of tribulation
    seem to drown us in despair.
A mother's love is a sanctuary
    where our souls can find sweet rest
From the struggle and the tension
    of life's fast and futile quest.
A mother's love is like a tower
    rising far above the crowd,
And her smile is like the sunshine
    breaking through a threatening cloud.

A mother's love is like a beacon
    burning bright with faith and prayer,
And through the changing scenes of life
    we find a haven there.
For a mother's love is fashioned
    after God's enduring love—
It is endless and unfailing
    like the love of Him above.

With
my love
so true,
And a kiss
or two

A Mother's Day Prayer

Our Father in heaven
    whose love is divine,
Thanks for the love
    of a mother like mine.
In Thy great mercy
    look down from above
And grant this dear mother
    the gift of Your love,
And all through the year,
    whatever betide her,
Assure her each day
    that You are beside her.
And, Father in heaven,
    show me the way
To lighten her tasks
    and brighten her day.
And bless her dear heart
    with the insight to see
That her love means more
    than the world to me.

If I should never see another miracle, my mother's love will have been enough.
GEORGE DOUGLAS

A Grandmother's Heart

On Mother's Day my thoughts go back
   to all the years that have gone before,
And all of my love and good wishes
   go straight to that open door.
For always the door to your heart and home
   stood open with welcoming cheer,
And memories of you, Grandmother,
   grow dearer with each year.

We cannot buy a quart of goodwill, a pound of love, or a yard of patience. We can only create such values from within ourselves by genuine effort. These are the values that build love and help make homes spiritually satisfying.

EDGAR N. JACKSON

To my Valentine

He Cares for You

Give thanks to the God of heaven.
His love endures forever.

PSALM 136:26

Trust to me

My Daily Prayer

God, be my resting place and my protection
    in hours of trouble, defeat, and dejection.
May I never give way to self-pity and sorrow,
    may I always be sure of a better tomorrow.
May I stand undaunted, come what may,
    secure in the knowledge I have only to pray
And ask my Creator and Father above
    to keep me serene in His grace and His love.

*For it is by grace you have been saved,
through faith—and this not from your-
selves, it is the gift of God—not by works,
so that no one can boast.*

EPHESIANS 2:8-9

The Gift of God's Love

It can't be bought,
  it can't be sold,
It can't be measured
  in silver and gold.
It's a special wish
  that God above
Will fill your heart
  with peace and love—
The love of God,
  which is divine,
That is beyond
  what words can define
So you may know
  the comfort of
God's all-fulfilling
  grace and love.

To fall in love with God is the greatest of all romances; to seek Him, the greatest adventure; to find Him, the greatest human achievement.

RAPHAEL SIMON

Somebody Cares

Somebody cares and always will—
    the world forgets, but God loves you still.
You cannot go beyond His love
    no matter what you're guilty of,
For God forgives until the end—
    He is your faithful, loyal friend.
And though you try to hide your face,
    there is no shelter any place
That can escape His watchful eye,
    for on the earth and in the sky
He's ever present and always there
    to take you in His tender care
And bind the wounds and mend the breaks
    when all the world around forsakes.
Somebody cares and loves you still,
    and God is the someone who always will.

*He loves each one of us, as if there
were only one of us.*

SAINT AUGUSTINE

84

The Love of God

The love of God

is too great to conceive.

Don't try to explain it—

just trust and believe!

I believe in God, in the same way in which I believe in my friends, because I feel the breath of His love and His invisible, intangible hand, bringing me here, carrying me there, pressing upon me.

MIGUEL DE UNAMUNO

85

Somebody Loves You

Somebody loves you more than you know,
   Somebody goes with you wherever you go,
Somebody really and truly cares
   and lovingly listens to all of your prayers.
Don't think for a minute that this is not true,
   for God loves His children and takes care of them too,
And all of His treasures are yours to share
   if you love Him completely and show that you care.
And if you walk in His footsteps and have faith to believe,
   there's nothing you ask for that you will not receive.

The earth is the LORD's and the fulness thereof,
the world and those who dwell therein;
for he has founded it upon the seas,
and established it upon the rivers.

PSALM 24:1 RSV

Meet God in the Morning

The earth is the Lord's,
   and the fulness thereof,
It speaks of His greatness,
   it sings of His love.
And each day at dawning,
   I lift my heart high
And raise up my eyes
   to the infinite sky.
I watch the night vanish
   as a new day is born,
And I hear the birds sing
   on the wings of the morn.

I see the dew glisten
   in crystal-like splendor
While God, with a touch
   that is gentle and tender,
Wraps up the night
   and softly tucks it away
And hangs out the sun
   to herald a new day.
And so I give thanks
   and my heart kneels to pray,
"God, keep me and guide me
   and go with me today."

*All the ways of the Lord are loving and faithful
for those who keep the demands of his covenant.*

PSALM 25:10

With Love.

Reflecting His Compassion

Life is not a holiday, but an education. And the one eternal lesson for us all is how better to love.

HENRY DRUMMOND

Strangers Are Friends We Haven't Met

God knows no strangers, He loves us all—
    the poor, the rich, the great, the small.
He is a friend who is always there
    to share our troubles and lessen our care.
For no one is a stranger in God's sight,
    for God is love, and in His light
May we, too, try in our small way
    to make new friends from day to day.
So pass no stranger with an unseeing eye,
    for God may be sending a new friend by.

Let brotherly love continue. Do not neglect to show hospitality to strangers, for thereby some have entertained angels unawares.

HEBREWS 13:1-2 RSV

To my Valentine.

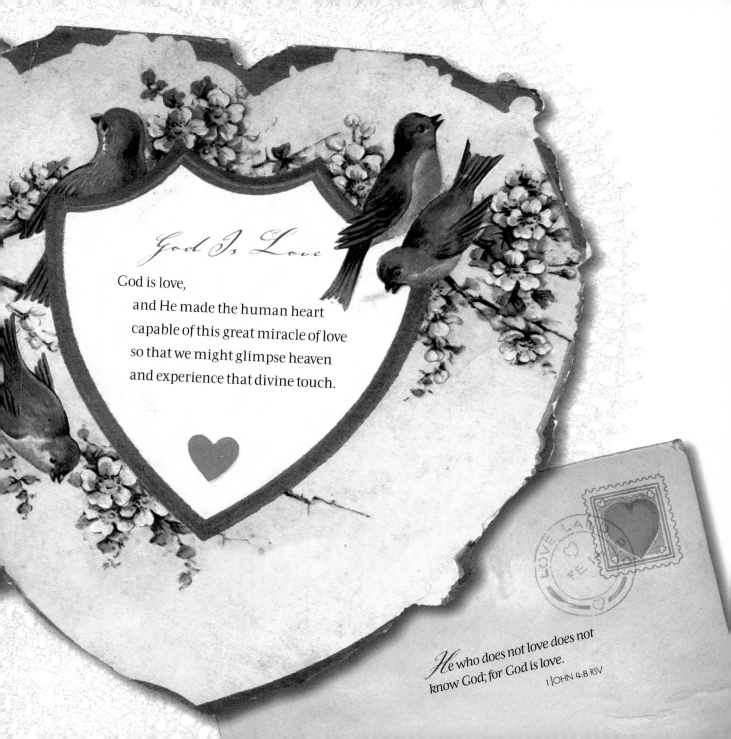

God Is Love

God is love,
    and He made the human heart
    capable of this great miracle of love
    so that we might glimpse heaven
    and experience that divine touch.

He who does not love does not
know God; for God is love.
1 JOHN 4:8 RSV

No Favor Do I Seek Today

I come not to ask, to plead, or implore You,
    I just come to tell You how much I adore You.
For to kneel in Your presence makes me feel blessed,
    for I know that You know all my needs best,
And it fills me with joy just to linger with You,
    As my soul You replenish and my heart You renew.
For prayer is much more than just asking for things—
    It's the peace and contentment that quietness brings.
So thank You again for Your mercy and love
    And for making me heir to Your kingdom above.

All can comprehend that a man is praying when he kneels down ... but all cannot understand that the highest prayer or communion with God is a life of love.

FREDERICK W. ROBERTSON

Good wishes

Grant Us Hope and Faith and Love

Hope for a world grown cynically cold,
    hungry for power and greedy for gold,
Faith to believe when, within and without,
    there's a nameless fear in a world of doubt,
Love that is bigger than race or creed
    to cover the world and fulfill each need ...
God grant these gifts of faith, hope, and love—
    three things this world has so little of—
For only these gifts from our Father above
    can turn our sins from hatred to love.

And now these three remain; faith, hope and love. But the greatest of these is love.

1 CORINTHIANS 13:13

A token of Affection

93

This Is All I Ask

Lord, show me the way I can somehow repay
  the blessings You've given me.
Lord, teach me to do what You most want me to
  and to be what You want me to be.
I'm unworthy, I know, but I do love You so,
  I beg You to answer my plea.
I've not much to give, but as long as I live
  may I give it completely to Thee.

God has a purpose for each one of us, a work for each one to do, a place for each one to fill, an influence for each one to exert, a likeness to His dear Son for each one to manifest, and then, a place for each one to fill in His holy temple.

ARTHUR C. A. HALL

Jesus said, "Let the little children come to me, and do not hinder them, for the kingdom of heaven belongs to such as these."

MATTHEW 19:14

Now I Lay Me Down to Sleep

I remember so well this prayer I said
Each night as my mother tucked me in bed,
And today this prayer is still the best way
To sign off with God at the end of the day
And to ask Him your soul to safely keep
As you wearily close your tired eyes in sleep,
Feeling content that the Father above
Will hold you secure in His great arms of love.
And having His promise if ere you wake
His angels reach down, your sweet soul to take
Is perfect assurance that, awake or asleep,
God is always right there to tenderly keep
All of His children ever safe in His care,
For God's here and He's there and He's everywhere.
So into His hands each night as I sleep
I commend my soul for the dear Lord to keep,
Knowing that if my soul should take flight
It will soar to the land where there is no night.

95

Dear God, You Are Love

Dear God, You are a part of me,
You're all I hear and all I see.
You're what I say and what I do
For all my life belongs to You.
You walk with me and You talk with me,
For I am Yours eternally.
And when I stumble, slip, and fall
Because I'm weak and lost and small,
You help me up and take my hand
And lead me toward the Promised Land.
I cannot dwell apart from You,
You would not ask or want me to,
For You have room within Your heart
To make each child of Yours a part
Of You and all Your love and care,
For You are love and love should be everywhere!

H.S.R.

To my Valentine

Thank You, Father,
for giving
love to the world.
Help me to make
Your gift
the basis of my living.

V.J.R.

To my Valentine